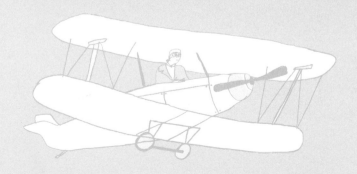

Amelia
EarHart

by Libby Romero

Illustrated by Charlotte Ager

Senior Editors Marie Greenwood, Roohi Sehgal
Designer Charlotte Jennings

Project Art Editor Roohi Rais
Jacket Coordinator Issy Walsh
Jacket Designer Dheeraj Arora
Senior DTP Designer Neeraj Bhatia
DTP Designer Sachin Gupta
Picture Researcher Rituraj Singh
Assistant Pre-Producer Abi Maxwell
Senior Producer Amy Knight
Managing Editors Laura Gilbert,
Monica Saigal, Jonathan Melmoth
Deputy Managing Art Editor Ivy Sengupta
Managing Art Editor Diane Peyton Jones
Delhi Team Head Malavika Talukder
Creative Director Helen Senior
Publishing Director Sarah Larter

Subject Consultant Lisa Cotham
Literacy Consultant Stephanie Laird

First American Edition, 2020
Published in the United States by DK Publishing
1450 Broadway, Suite 801, New York, NY 10018

Copyright © 2020 Dorling Kindersley Limited
DK, a Division of Penguin Random House LLC
20 21 22 23 24 10 9 8 7 6 5 4 3 2 1
001–316566–Feb/2020

A catalog record for this book is available from the Library of Congress.
ISBN: 978-1-4654-9066-7 (Paperback)
ISBN: 978-1-4654-9067-4 (Hardcover)

DK books are available at special discounts when purchased
in bulk for sales promotions, premiums, fund-raising, or educational use.
For details, contact: DK Publishing Special Markets,
1450 Broadway, Suite 801, New York, NY 10018
SpecialSales@dk.com

Printed and bound in China

A WORLD OF IDEAS:
SEE ALL THERE IS TO KNOW

www.dk.com

Amelia EarHart

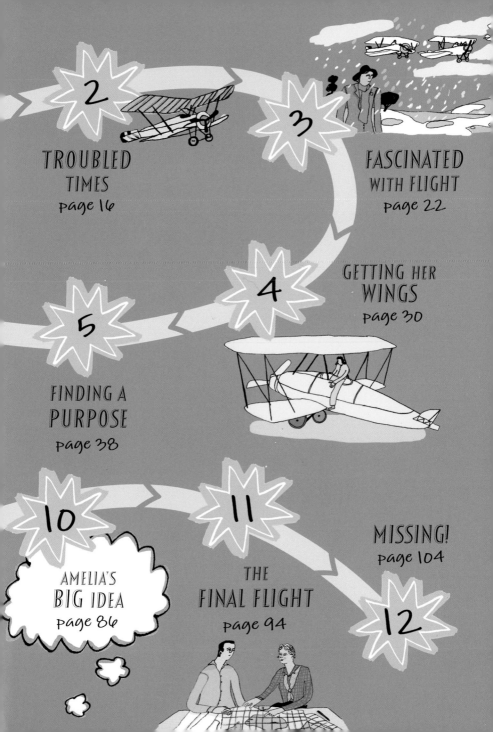

Chapter 1

The **kid** from **Kansas**

On July 24, 1897, Amelia Mary Earhart—who would one day capture hearts around the world—made her first appearance.

She was born in the southwest bedroom on the second floor of her grandparents' home in Atchison, Kansas. It was a large house sitting high above the Missouri River and a symbol of the family's wealth. Amelia's grandparents, Alfred and Amelia Otis, were two of the first Atchison settlers. It was there that Amelia's mother, Amy, grew up, pampered, adored, and protected.

Amelia's father, Edwin, on the other hand, was the youngest son of a preacher.

The life of...
Amelia **Earhart**

Dear Reader,

Many people remember Amelia Earhart as the woman who disappeared when she tried to fly around the world. That may be true, but it's rather sad that this last act ... a tragic accident ... is what people recollect most, for Amelia Earhart was so much more.

During her lifetime, Amelia was an early pioneer in aviation. She set many height, speed, and distance records in her planes. She was also a social worker, fashion designer, celebrity, teacher, lecturer, nurse, role model, businesswoman, and an outspoken advocate for women's rights.

Amelia used people's fascination with her achievements to promote her strong belief that women were just as capable as men. She believed that everyone—men and women—should have the courage to chase their dreams. If they stumbled, failure was a challenge to try again. To her, fun was a reason to do something, and the adventure in itself was worthwhile. Even today, we could all learn something from Amelia.

Happy reading,
Libby Romero

Although highly regarded among his parishioners, Edwin's father, the Reverend David Earhart, and his wife, Mary, struggled to make ends meet. Despite these difficult circumstances, Edwin showed early promise and went on to study law in Kansas. There, he met Amy and they quickly fell in love and decided to get married. Amy's father, however, did not approve of the match.

He wanted Amy to marry someone in their own social circle. He told Edwin that he had to prove himself and earn a stable income. So Edwin did just that. He worked steadily for years, and, finally, Amy's father allowed them to marry.

DID YOU KNOW?

As per family tradition, Amelia was named after her two grandmothers, Amelia Harres Otis and Mary Wells Earhart.

Alfred even bought the couple a home in Kansas City, Kansas. But he still did not like or trust his new son-in-law.

Amelia spent the first three years of her life living with her parents in their Kansas City home. Then, after the birth of Amelia's younger sister, Muriel, it was agreed that Amelia should live with her grandparents in Atchison. Amelia's grandmother, now 60, was lonely. Edwin traveled a lot with his job, so the arrangement would also help Amelia's mother, who had her hands full with the new baby.

And so began a split life for Amelia. For most of the year she lived in Atchison, but each summer, she returned to her parents' home in Kansas City.

Amelia with her little sister, Muriel

For the most part, Amelia was happy living with her grandparents. Her bedroom had a view overlooking the Missouri River. The house had a large library, which provided plenty of reading material. Amelia was able to read by the time she was five. However, while Amelia's parents tried to encourage her to be curious and try new things, her grandmother insisted on traditional "ladylike" behavior. Keeping Grandma Otis happy was a challenge for an adventurous girl like Amelia, but it didn't stop her from having fun.

Once, Grandma Otis got angry with Amelia for climbing over a fence instead of passing through the gate. Amelia never forgot how her grandma made her feel, and she knew that if she had been a boy her behavior would have been considered perfectly normal.

In Atchison, Amelia had a close-knit group of friends consisting of cousins Lucy (Toot) and Kathryn (Katch) Challis, who lived next door, and Virginia (Ginger) Park, who lived two blocks away. On the many occasions when Muriel visited, she joined the group, too.

With Amelia leading the way, the girls rode horses and bikes, went roller skating, and climbed trees. They had mud ball fights and played baseball, basketball, and football with the boys.

GIRL STUFF

Amelia liked to play sports, but back then exercising was not something girls were encouraged to do. Even their clothes got in the way, since girls typically wore dresses made of fabrics that tore quite easily. One summer, Amelia's mother had a seamstress make bloomers (loose pants) for her daughters to wear when they played outside. Amelia loved her bloomers, even though they shocked the little girls who wore dresses.

They also went on picnics, took imaginary trips around the world in a game they invented called Bogie, and explored the many caves along the bluffs of the Missouri River. Amelia's grandmother, of course, did not know about these adventures.

Amelia's parents were much less strict than Grandmother Otis. So in Kansas City, Amelia and Muriel got to do whatever they wanted—ladylike or not. Their father took them fishing, and at Christmas he bought them toys that were intended for boys.

What are bluffs?   Bluffs are high, steep cliffs that overlook rivers, beaches, or other coastal areas.

During the winter, the girls liked to go sledding. At the top of one big hill, Amelia—seeking more speed—chose to ride a boys' flat sled, which required lying on one's belly, instead of a girls' sled, which had a seat. As she raced down the hill, the junkman's cart pulled directly in her path. Amelia slid right between the horse's front and back legs. Lying down may have saved her life!

One of Amelia's most daring exploits came after she and her family traveled to the 1904 St. Louis World's Fair. Amelia rode the Ferris wheel with her father, but her mother refused to let her ride the roller coaster, saying it was too dangerous for a young girl. When Amelia returned to Atchison, she built her own roller coaster. It was fun—until Grandma Otis made her take it down.

"Unfortunately, I lived at a time when girls were still girls."

Amelia Earhart, in her autobiography, *The Fun of It*, 1932

15

Troubled times

Up to now, Amelia's biggest worry had been figuring out how to keep Grandma Otis happy. That would soon change.

In 1908, Amelia's father got a new job and the family moved to Des Moines, Iowa. This move was the beginning of the end of Amelia's happy childhood.

Amelia's life had been centered in Atchison with her grandparents, so the move meant leaving everyone she loved and everything she knew.

But for her father, the new job with the Chicago, Rock Island, and Pacific Railroad line was a welcome opportunity. It paid more than his

last job and, even with the required move, seemed to be the best choice for the family.

At first, Edwin flourished. At home, he was a wonderful father who not only told fantastic stories but also acted them out with his daughters and the neighborhood children. At work, he did such a good job that within a year he was promoted, and he got four raises in four years. Each time, the family moved to a bigger and better home in a more fashionable part of town.

It was at this time that Amelia saw an airplane for the first time, at the Iowa State Fair in Des Moines. She was 10 years old. Unimpressed, she said it was "a thing of rusty wire and wood and looked not at all interesting."

Two years later, however, things were different because Amelia's father started to change. He spent money he didn't have, he became unhappy in his marriage, and he began to drink alcohol. At first, it was just a little. Then, it was a lot.  Amelia, Muriel, and their mother tried to hide the problem from everyone, but after Edwin stumbled home drunk one afternoon— in front of all the neighborhood children—that became impossible. Everyone knew their secret.

Amelia's grandparents tried to convince her mother to leave him. When she refused, they changed their wills. Worried that Edwin would spend everything Amy had, they locked Amy's inheritance into a trust. Amy's brother, Mark, was put in charge of her money, and she wouldn't receive anything until 15 years after her parents' deaths.

| **what is alcohol?** | Alcohol is a strong drink such as beer, wine, or whiskey. If people drink too much alcohol, it can change their mood or cause health problems. |

Eventually, Edwin's drinking caused him to lose his job. When word of Edwin's problem spread throughout the railroad industry, nobody wanted to hire him. After a year, he finally found a low-level job working as a freight clerk in St. Paul, Minnesota. It was the spring of 1913, and the family had to move again.

The Earharts moved into a new house that was large but shabby. They couldn't afford to buy enough coal to heat all of it in the winter so they closed off half the rooms to stay warm.

Amelia, now a junior, and Muriel, a freshman, attended the St. Paul Central High School. Amelia liked the school's wide variety of challenging courses, and she enrolled in physics, Latin, German, and math. She even joined the girls' basketball team. But life at home was difficult and the strain of that took a toll on Amelia's grades, which dropped.

One outlet the sisters did have was their church, which became a major part of their social lives. Amelia sang in the choir and joined the Altar Guild, a group that ran errands, cleaned, and did whatever else needed to be done for the church.

The next spring, Edwin announced that he had found a new job, so the family packed up again and set off for Springfield, Missouri. But when they got there, there was no job. They spent the night in a boarding house by the tracks. Then Amy made a decision: it was time to leave Edwin. She and the girls were moving to Chicago.

Amelia wanted to go to Hyde Park, the best high school in the city. To do that, they had to live in the expensive Hyde Park neighborhood, so her mother rented a couple of rooms in an apartment there. The rooms were miserable, but they were the only thing Amy could afford.

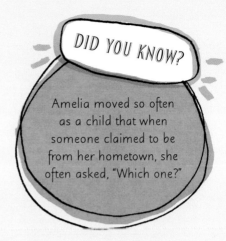

Hyde Park High School offered dozens of clubs and even sports teams for girls. However, Amelia, now a senior, didn't join anything. Instead, she spent most of her free time in the library. Amelia didn't have any friends and she didn't try to fit in. She didn't even go to her high school graduation.

Fascinated WITH flight

After Amelia graduated from high school, several things happened that would have a big impact on her life and that of her family.

It all started with her father, who had stopped drinking and moved to Kansas City to live with his sister. In the fall of 1915, Amelia, her mother, and her sister moved there, too. The family was still poor, but Amelia's father was able to practice law again.

His first case was battling Amy's brother, Mark, for control of his wife's inheritance—and he won. This meant Amy could now afford to send Amelia to college. Amelia enrolled in the Ogontz School for Young Ladies in Philadelphia—one of the most exclusive schools in the country. This appealed to Amelia's mother, who saw the school as a way to rebuild Amelia's—and the family's—social standing after years of living in poverty. During her first year at Ogontz, Amelia excelled in her studies and in sports, which—to her delight—were not only encouraged but also required by the school's headmistress. While at Ogontz, Amelia was put under the charge of her aunt, Margaret, who lived nearby. And she did keep her aunt busy! Aunt Margaret was called to the school several times because Amelia had been caught climbing on the roofs.

DID YOU KNOW?

Amelia was such a good field hockey player that she was invited to join Alpha Phi, a secret athletic society at Ogontz.

Unlike the school administrators, Amelia didn't think that getting married was the "ideal vocation" for a woman. So, as her horizons broadened, she began to think more and more about her future. She even started collecting newspaper and magazine clippings about women in exciting male-dominated careers, such as engineers, activists, movie producers, and even an industrial psychologist. Amelia pasted the stories into a scrapbook, which she called "Activities of Women."

During her sophomore year, Amelia was elected vice president of her class and became secretary of the Ogontz Red Cross, an organization the school had set up after the US entered World War I. Each day, members spent one class period knitting sweaters for Allied troops.

what is the Ogontz Red Cross?

It is a chapter, or local branch, of the Red Cross, a volunteer organization that helps people facing emergencies around the world.

WORLD WAR I

World War I was an international conflict that began on July 28, 1914. During the war, the Allies (mainly Great Britain, France, Russia, Japan, Canada, Italy, and later the US) fought the Central Powers of Germany, Austria-Hungary, and Turkey. Soldiers on both sides dug long, narrow trenches where they often battled for weeks at a time. The war ended on November 11, 1918, after the two sides signed an armistice, or agreement to stop fighting. More than 18 million people died during the war.

They also collected food and money to donate to the Red Cross.

That Christmas, Amelia and her mother went to visit Muriel, who was now studying in Toronto, Canada. The US had been in the war for a few months, but Canada had been fighting for three years. Everywhere Amelia went, she saw war veterans who had lost arms, legs, or their sight. Feeling utterly useless, Amelia made a sudden decision— she was going to leave school to help out.

Amelia moved to Toronto and started taking classes to become a nurse's aide. She worked in a hospital until the war ended.

When Amelia had free time, she often headed to the stables. One day when she was out horseback riding, three Air Force officers invited her to watch them take off and land in their planes at the airfield. Amelia was awestruck by the big, beautiful machines. To her, they looked like full-sized birds sliding on the snow. She listened to their roar as it echoed off the trees, and she stood so close to the planes that their propellers threw snow in her face.

NURSE'S AIDE

During World War I, women were given few opportunities to actively participate in the war. Some, like Amelia, became nurse's aides through the Red Cross's Volunteer Aid Detachment (VAD) program. As a VAD volunteer, Amelia's jobs included scrubbing floors, playing tennis with able patients, helping in the kitchen, and handing out medicines.

For the first time, Amelia felt an urge to fly. She tried to get permission to go up in a plane, but not even a plea to the general's wife could make that happen. Instead, Amelia got to know the fliers and listened to their stories.

Amelia grew even more interested in flying after she and a friend went to a Toronto fair and saw a stunt flying exhibition.

In the air above her, Amelia saw military ace pilots perform daring stunts with their planes. The planes climbed and turned, they zoomed and banked, they stalled and came rushing toward the ground. The skilled pilots put on a show the crowd would never forget.

AEROBATICS

In the 1920s, stunt pilots traveled the country, thrilling people with their dangerous tricks in the air, called aerial maneuvers. Popular stunts included the loop, roll, and spin.

A loop is a vertical circle in the air. The cockpit can point inward (inside loop) or out of the loop (outside loop).

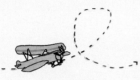

During a roll, an airplane rolls to the left or right and completes a circle as it flies straight ahead.

In a spin, a plane rotates on its axis as it flies straight down. Pilots need to be very high up in the air to complete a spin.

The girls wanted a better view of the aerial loops, rolls, and spins, so they stood in the middle of a large clearing. Then one pilot swooped down toward the crowd and dove right toward them. Amelia's friend ran, but Amelia stood her ground, fascinated by the little red airplane.

In 1918, the worldwide flu pandemic known as the "Spanish flu" swept through North America, claiming Amelia as one of its victims. She was so sick that she needed surgery to drain the infection

from her sinus cavity. During her long recovery, Amelia decided she wanted to become a doctor, and when she was well enough, she enrolled at the College of Physicians and Surgeons at Columbia University in New York City.

Soon afterward, however, Amelia changed her mind, deciding she was more suited to medical research. Perhaps by choice—or maybe due to the persistent pleadings of her parents, who had now reunited—Amelia moved to Los Angeles to live with them. She planned to enroll in college there in the fall, but that never happened. Instead, as she put it: "aviation caught me."

4

Getting her wings

In the 1920s, flying was the new craze on the West Coast. Soon after their arrival in Los Angeles, Amelia and her father attended an air meet.

Finding a meet wasn't difficult. New airfields were popping up everywhere, and each weekend at least one of them hosted an event. Amelia, of course, went to the area's biggest, busiest, and most famous airfield for her first meet. Massive airships floated through the air. Daring performers walked on airplane wings—sometimes moving from one plane to another—as the planes flew through the sky. Some airplanes flipped and turned as the pilots completed aerial tricks.

Death-defying stunts like this made American wing-walker Lillian Boyer famous.

Others streaked toward the finish line of the featured races. The weather was perfect, the show was exciting, and Amelia was absolutely captivated by what she saw.

Amelia wanted more. She got her father to take her to more air meets, and soon she convinced him to pay for her first flight, a 10-minute trip that cost $10. Like most pilots at the time, the man who flew her plane, Frank Hawks, had been a fighter pilot during the war. And like most people at the time, he didn't think a woman would be brave enough to go up in the air.

WHO WAS FRANK HAWKS?

Frank Hawks was one of the most famous air race pilots in the world. During his career, he set 214 point-to-point speed records in the US and Europe. Hawks retired from speed racing in 1937 and became a salesman for a small airplane manufacturer. He died one year later when he and a potential client were killed in an accident shortly after takeoff. He was 41 years old.

He refused to take Amelia on the flight unless another pilot went with them—to hold her in the plane in case she decided to jump out!

However, Frank had nothing to fear. As soon as the plane took off, Amelia knew she wanted to learn how to fly. In fact, she felt like she would die if she didn't! That evening, she shared her plans with her family. Both her parents expressed an interest, and her father even asked when she planned to start taking lessons.

A few days later, Amelia announced that she had signed up for lessons and needed help paying for them. Her father was shocked. He hadn't thought she was serious! He figured Amelia would drop the idea if he didn't give her any money, so he told her they couldn't afford the lessons. Instead, Amelia went out and got a job as a mail clerk at the local telephone company and paid for the lessons herself.

Frank, who took Amelia on her first flight, was one of the best pilots around. But Amelia didn't like his ideas about female pilots and decided to take lessons from a woman instead. She signed up for classes with 24-year-old Neta Snook, the only

Neta (left) with Amelia

female instructor in southern California. Neta agreed to teach Amelia on credit until she had enough money to make regular monthly payments.

A DANGEROUS OCCUPATION

Flying in the 1920s was extremely dangerous. Airplane motors quit midair and propellers would suddenly stop turning. Plus, there weren't many landing strips, so pilots tried to land wherever they could—often crashing their planes in the process. Even the best pilots weren't guaranteed that they would be alive at the end of the day. For Amelia, this risk was part of the attraction.

Amelia showed up for her first lesson on January 3, 1921, in her horseback riding outfit. The outfit, which became her signature look, was practical. The jacket protected her from wind and dust, and the jodhpurs and boots made it easier to climb into the cockpit. Neta's plane had two open cockpits, each with a matching set of controls. For their first lesson, the two women taxied around the runway, with Neta moving the rudder bar and stick and Amelia copying each action. Neta, being the instructor, sat in the back where she could correct any mistakes Amelia made.

It rained a lot that winter, and by the end of February Amelia had only been able to log four hours of flight time.

Amelia in her horseback riding outfit.

When Amelia started flying, she had long hair, in keeping with the fashion of the day—a look she wanted to maintain so people didn't think she was eccentric. Being a female pilot (aviatrix) was odd enough! However, she cut her hair into a bob after a young girl told her she didn't look like an aviatrix because of her long hair. As for the curls for which Amelia was famous, they were courtesy of a curling iron. Amelia's hair was naturally straight.

Although Amelia was a confident flier, she still had a lot to learn. Despite this, Amelia had decided that it was time for her to have her own plane and she knew exactly which one she wanted: the little Airster that the airstrip's owner, Bert Kinner, had just built. It was smaller and faster than Neta's plane, and it was painted bright yellow.

Despite Neta's objections that Amelia wasn't ready for such a small plane, Amelia convinced her family to loan her enough money to buy the aircraft just before her 24th birthday. She named it "the Canary."

Neta volunteered to teach Amelia how to fly the plane for free, but soon the two women clashed. Neta thought Amelia had now logged enough time to attempt a solo flight. Amelia, however, refused because she didn't feel ready. Then they had two minor crashes, and Amelia decided to switch instructors.

Amelia wanted to be able to control her plane in any situation, so she began working with John Montijo, an ex-army pilot, who taught her stunt flying. She practiced the moves until they became second nature.

Within a few months, Amelia took her first solo flight, and by the end of the year she was participating in air meets, often as the featured attraction.

In the air, things were going well for
Amelia. Her exploits in the Canary were
frequently reported in the newspapers,
particularly after she set a new women's
altitude record at more than
14,000 ft (4,300 m). In 1923,
Amelia became the 16th woman
to earn a pilot's license from the
Fédération Aéronautique Internationale,
an international aviation organization.

But at home, things were getting rocky
again. Amelia's parents were having more
financial problems and took in boarders to
get by. Among their boarders was a man
named Sam Chapman, and he and Amelia
began dating. Even with the extra income from
boarders, the family struggled financially.
Amelia sold her plane and started looking for
a full-time job to help support her family.

Finding a **purpose**

Grounded and broke, Amelia began her job search. She didn't want just any job—she wanted something interesting.

Amelia also wanted something that would leave her plenty of time for flying. First, she tried photography. She sold at least one roll of film containing photos of a gushing oil well, but she soon realized that this particular career didn't have the moneymaking potential she sought.

Next, Amelia attempted to cash in on the building boom that was turning southern California's open fields into massive subdivisions. She and a local mechanic bought a big truck and started a hauling business. This was an unconventional career for a woman at the time, but the business was profitable enough for Amelia to begin saving money for a new plane.

In 1924, Amelia's parents decided to get divorced and the family split up for good. Edwin stayed in California, and everyone else—including Amelia's boyfriend, Sam—decided to move back East

DID YOU KNOW?

Amelia liked to take photos of ordinary objects in unusual ways. She was particularly fond of garbage cans.

to the Boston area. Instead of buying another airplane, Amelia bought a little yellow sportscar, which she called "Canary," to drive her mother to Boston. To give her mother time to recover from the pain of her divorce, Amelia didn't head straight for Boston. Instead, she and her mother took a 7,000-mile (11,000-km) round-about trip, visiting a host of national parks along the way. Amelia didn't mind driving. Her sinus infection had returned, so it would have been very painful to make the trip by plane.

By the time they joined Muriel in Boston,

Amelia's sinus infection was so bad that she had to undergo more surgery. It took months for her to recover, but eventually Amelia felt well enough to move to New York.

Her goal now was to become an engineer. Amelia re-enrolled in Columbia University and took two classes—elementary physics and intermediate algebra. However, she didn't have enough money to keep studying, and withdrew before the semester ended. Even so, she passed physics, but the C- she got in algebra meant she got no credit for that course.

Amelia enrolled in a Harvard summer program to make up the credit. Then, she applied to the Massachusetts Institute of Technology (MIT). However, she couldn't afford to go there without a scholarship, which she didn't get, so Amelia moved back to Boston to live with her mother and sister.

The Boston skyline over the Boston Public Garden

For the first time in her life, Amelia had no plan. Every time she tried to pursue a formal education, money—or rather, lack of it—got in the way. Amelia needed a job. She started tutoring blind men in trigonometry (the study of triangles) and then she worked as a nurse's companion in a hospital for people with mental illnesses.

Fortunately, Amelia was in Boston—a city that had a history of fostering success in women. One day, she went to the Women's Educational and Industrial Union (WEIU), a guidance center run by women, looking for help. Charmed by Amelia's personality and confidence, the interviewer overlooked her lack of experience and sent her to Denison House, one of the oldest settlement houses in the country. Here, Amelia would train to become a social worker.

Initially, Amelia taught English and citizenship classes to adults. Soon, she was put in charge of several children's groups where she taught girls how to play basketball and to fence. Initially hired on a part-time basis, Amelia became a full-time employee within a year and moved into Denison House. Meanwhile, Sam, who was now Amelia's fiancé, was still

WHAT WAS DENISON HOUSE?

Denison House was a settlement house that provided educational support and a variety of activities and services in a rundown, lower-class part of Boston. It was a beacon for social change as well as a haven for the area's large poor and immigrant population. Most employees were middle- or upper-middle-class, college-educated women who used their skills and network of social contacts to enrich the lives of the people they served.

patiently waiting for
Amelia to settle down
and marry him. Amelia was
gaining her personal and
financial independence, and a future as a social
worker was within her grasp. However, flying
was still her dream.

Amelia wasn't earning enough to buy another
airplane, but she still took flights as a passenger.
One day as she was flying over the city, Amelia
tossed out free passes to an upcoming Denison
House fundraising event. The press pounced
on it, garnering publicity for both Amelia and
the event. And when Amelia signed on as a
part-time director of a new Boston airfield,
reporters pounced on that, too. Female pilots
and achievers were touted broadly and loudly
in the Boston press.

THEA RASCHE

Thea Rasche (1899–1971) was the first German woman to obtain a pilot's license after World War I. A few months later she earned her aerobatic license, and soon she became the most famous female stunt flier in Europe. Her stunts, including flying under New York City's Brooklyn Bridge, were so daring that the press called her "Dare-Devil of the Skies." Other female pilots called her "Queen of the Air."

In September of 1927, Amelia went to an air show to watch the performance of Thea Rasche, the leading female stunt flier. Midway through the routine, the plane's engine died. Thea came in for a landing, only to see that she was headed straight toward a crowd of people. She slid into a swamp instead.

Amelia jumped into an airplane and put on a performance of her own. Her boss thought she was just filling in the time, but Amelia had another reason. She knew Thea couldn't avoid landing in the swamp. She also knew the press would use this as evidence that women shouldn't fly airplanes. Amelia went up in the air to prove that women were just as capable as pilots and as daring as men.

Crossing THE Atlantic

In the spring of 1927, American pilot Charles Lindbergh became the first person to fly solo across the Atlantic Ocean.

One year later, Amelia got a phone call that would change her life forever. Since Lindbergh's crossing, sponsors had been offering pilots huge prizes to tackle aerial "firsts." One of the biggest contests was to be the first woman to repeat Lindbergh's trip. Five women had already

Charles Lindbergh before his transatlantic flight

tried—three died, one had to be rescued, and one never got off the ground. Now, out of the blue, Amelia was going to get her chance, thanks to a woman named Amy Phipps Guest.

Amy had never flown before, but that wasn't going to stop this wealthy 55-year-old socialite from trying. She bought a plane, which she named the *Friendship*, from Commander Richard E. Byrd, a friend of hers who had flown around the North Pole. Byrd was also helping her plan her expedition. She hired the pilot and co-pilot of her choosing. But the one thing her fortune couldn't buy was her family's approval, and when they found out what she was up to they begged her not to do it.

AMY'S INSPIRATION

One reason Amy Guest tried to become the first woman to fly across the Atlantic was to prevent another woman—Mabel Boll—from capturing the honor. Mabel was a publicity-seeking adventurer who earned her nickname, the "Queen of Diamonds," for her habit of flashing massive diamond rings everywhere she went. Amy couldn't bear the thought of Mabel becoming the most famous woman in the world. To ensure Mabel didn't succeed, Amy bought the plane and hired the pilot that Mabel had lined up for the trip.

Amy Phipps Guest

Mabel Boll

Amy was grounded ... but she was determined to see another American woman tackle the feat. She asked her lawyer to find a female pilot. It was a chance encounter that put Amelia on Amy's radar. Shortly after the lawyer started searching for a female pilot, publisher George Palmer Putnam met a pilot. He told George that a wealthy woman

George Palmer
Putnam

had bought Byrd's plane and was planning a long flight.

Recognizing the potential for a great story, George asked his friend Hilton Railey, a public relations specialist, to track down the woman. Hilton found her lawyer instead, and George called him. The lawyer needed help finding a female pilot, so George asked around and found Amelia.

The next day, Amelia got a phone call from Hilton. He asked if she would be interested in doing something for aviation that might be hazardous. Hilton didn't reveal much, but it was enough for Amelia to be intrigued. After two interviews, they realized Amelia was exactly what they wanted—college-educated, dignified, attractive, and a pilot. Amy invited her to go on the flight.

The *Friendship* was in Boston, where Amelia lived, but she wasn't allowed to go anywhere near the plane in case the press or potential competitors figured out what the group was planning. If anyone questioned why the plane was undergoing modifications, their cover story was that Byrd was planning a South Pole expedition.

In the hangar, the *Friendship* was fitted with pontoons so it could take off and land on water.

THE FRIENDSHIP

The *Friendship* was a Fokker Trimotor airplane, one of the fastest, most reliable planes of its day. It was the first Fokker equipped with pontoons (floats) and the first airplane with pontoons to attempt an Atlantic Ocean crossing. Pontoons give pilots a better chance of surviving if they land at sea, but they also reduce a plane's flying speed. That makes it difficult to take off with a heavy load. And with the extra gas and equipment the team installed, the *Friendship* was a very heavy plane.

FRIENDSHIP

Pontoon

Two large fuel tanks were installed in the cabin to hold the 900 extra gallons (3,400 liters) of gasoline they would need to make the trip. The plane's wings were painted bright gold and its fuselage (body) orange—colors that would make it easy to spot if they went down at sea. All of the latest aviation equipment was installed to give the crew the best chance of success.

Amelia was not trained to use all of the aircraft's new equipment, so she wouldn't be flying the plane herself—this was the job of pilot Wilmer "Bill" Stultz. They would be joined by mechanic Lou Gordon.

Photos of Amelia, which would later earn her the nickname "Lady Lindy" because of her perceived similarity to Charles Lindbergh, were shot in secret.

DID YOU KNOW?

Amelia was captain of the *Friendship*, but she wasn't allowed to fly the plane.

One of Amelia's last tasks was to write a brief will, along with farewell letters to her mother, father, and sister. Her fiancé, Sam, was put in charge of telling her mother if something happened and Amelia didn't come back.

Finally, everything was in place. The only obstacle now was the weather, which kept the *Friendship* in Boston the first two times the crew tried to take off. Then, on June 3, the weather cleared and the *Friendship* headed up the coast, only to encounter thick fog. Instruments for flying blind hadn't been invented yet, so when they spotted an opening in the fog over Halifax, Nova Scotia, the crew set down.

The next day, they flew to Trepassey, Newfoundland. But news of their expedition had gotten out. Major newspapers ran stories about the Boston girl starting her Atlantic trip. Even worse, the weather took hold again. Day after day, Amelia and her crew tried to leave.

what does flying blind mean?

Flying blind means to fly an airplane when visibility is extremely low. Pilots rely on the plane's instruments, not their sight, to guide them.

But fog and strong winds prevented the heavy plane from lifting off. Meanwhile, the competition was closing in. Mabel Boll and Thea Rasche were planning to start their own transatlantic trips within days.

On June 17, despite continuing bad weather, Amelia decided they had to leave. The plane still wouldn't lift off the water, so they started dumping cans of gasoline into the harbor to reduce its weight. Finally, with just 700 gallons (2,650 liters) of fuel left to make the 20-hour trip, the *Friendship* started to climb.

They were off, only to be plagued by bad weather once again. Fog ... snow ... thunderstorms ... the *Friendship* weathered all of this before briefly reaching clear skies. Bill contacted two ships to get their bearings.

They were only 10 miles (16 km) off course. Then, the fog, which was to be their companion for 19 hours of their trip, closed in again.

Tucked away in the cabin, Amelia fell asleep. When she awoke she learned that the radio had stopped working. Bill knew they were near Ireland, so he nosed the plane down and they spotted a ship through breaks in the clouds. Unable to reach the ship via radio, they began circling it in the hope that crewmembers would paint the latitude and longitude on the ship's deck—a common practice at the time.

Boston

Halifax

Trepassey

Burry Port

But nobody noticed them. Amelia tied
messages to oranges and dropped them
toward the ship. She missed and soon
ran out of oranges.

Refusing to give up and not
wanting to waste any more fuel,
Bill flew on. Soon after, they
spotted land. The engines
started to cough and sputter. Bill found a bay
and set down. They had arrived at Burry Port,
Wales, just south of the Irish coast. Miraculously,
they were just one mile off course! They had
been flying for 20 hours, 40 minutes and they
were completely out of gas.

7

Instant celebrity

Amelia was merely a passenger and she hadn't flown the _Friendship_. Nobody cared. Upon landing she became the most famous woman in the world.

Rather than leaving the plane immediately, Amelia waited on the _Friendship_ until Hilton Railey and a _New York Times_ reporter could join them. Oblivious to the crowd gathering on shore, she used that time to compose a newspaper article she was obligated to write about her adventure.

By the time the _Friendship_ crew arrived in London the next day, Amelia's tale was splashed across the front page of _The New York Times_ and _The Times_ in London. George Putnam's master plan to make her a star was well underway.

Amelia is welcomed in London, England, after her flight from Newfoundland to Wales in June, 1928.

Calvin Coolidge

Despite Amelia's protests that the pilot, Bill, had done all the work, people focused on her. Reporters around the globe wrote about the first woman to cross the Atlantic—and her companions. US President Calvin Coolidge sent Amelia a congratulatory telegram. Automaker Henry Ford put a limousine at her disposal. Amelia was invited to give speeches, attend dinners and teas, and visit both the American embassy in London and the British Houses of Parliament. And for the first time, she met her sponsor, Amy Guest.

While in England, Amelia also bought a new plane from Lady Mary Heath, a famous British aviatrix. It was small, fast, easy to handle, and its

wings could be folded up for easy storage. It could fly long distances, too—Lady Mary had used it to fly from Croydon, England, to Cape Town, South Africa, and back. Amelia had the plane shipped back to the US.

In late June, the *Friendship* crew set sail for the United States, and arrived in New York City on July 6. There they were greeted with parades and celebrations and were given medals in cities such as New York, Boston, and Chicago. People everywhere wanted Amelia to visit.

Amelia knew she was only being given extra attention because she was a woman. She tried to promote everyone else involved in the venture and she talked about settlement houses and social work whenever she could. Her hope was to return to Denison House when the hubbub died down, but it didn't take long for her to realize that her fame now made it impossible for her to return to her prior life.

Amelia's book tells the story of her epic flight.

So, Amelia began to tackle her next obligation instead. She had to write a book about her trip. For three weeks in July, Amelia retreated to George and Dorothy Putnam's estate in Rye, New York, and set to work. Centering the tale on logbook entries she had recorded during the *Friendship*'s flight, Amelia wrote a book called *20 hrs. 40 min.: Our Flight in the Friendship*. George published the book immediately.

George was an excellent promoter. He packed Amelia's schedule with speeches, ribbon-cutting ceremonies, and other events, making sure to have a reporter and photographer present each time. All this publicity kept Amelia's name in the headlines, but sometimes George's strategy backfired.

DID YOU KNOW?

Amelia dedicated her book about the *Friendship*'s flight to Dorothy Putnam.

For example, after getting Amelia to endorse *Lucky Strike* cigarettes, a deal to have her write for the family-based *McCall's* magazine fell through because the magazine did not approve of smoking. But that just opened the door for Amelia to become an aviation editor for *Cosmopolitan* magazine instead.

The Putnams had become Amelia's constant companions, escorting her wherever she went. For the most part, this went smoothly, but occasionally Amelia took things into her own hands. Once she fled from a sweltering limousine and hopped into the sidecar of a police motorcycle, convincing the officer to rush through the city, siren blaring, and take her back to the Putnam estate.

There was one big complication: George was falling in love with Amelia, and Dorothy was very aware of what was happening. So was Amelia.

Amelia's life was now full of activity and distractions. She was now financially independent and ready to tackle a goal she had first set in 1924: to fly across the US And so, on August 31, 1928—without a plan and with George in the passenger seat—Amelia left New York and headed for Pittsburgh, Pennsylvania.

Everything went fine until it came time to land. Airplane engines were more reliable than they had been just a few years before, but landing strips were not. Amelia tried to set down on a runway surrounded by rocks, stumps, and ditches. Her plane rolled into a shallow ditch hidden in the grass and flipped over.

Neither Amelia nor George were hurt, but the plane's propeller was broken and its landing gear was cracked. Once the plane was fixed, Amelia was off again. George went back to New York.

This was Amelia's first long-distance solo flight, and one of the biggest challenges she faced was navigation. Because aviation was such a new industry, aerial maps (based on photographs taken from the air) did not exist. Amelia had to rely on road maps to make her way across the country instead. This meant she had to fly low enough to identify landmarks, and she had to pin the map to her pants to keep it from blowing away, as her plane had an open cockpit.

Whatever Amelia lacked in technology or experience, she more than made up for with luck and charm. Wherever she landed, people were more than happy to do whatever they could to help her out. One day, just before darkness fell, Amelia landed on Main Street in Hobbs, New Mexico. The curious townsfolk gave her gas

for her plane, food for
her belly, and a place to
sleep for the night. They
also found a place for
her to store her plane.

The next day, Amelia
set off again and she finally arrived in Los
Angeles on September 14. Two weeks later, she
flew back over the Rockies and headed home.
She had just become the first woman to fly
from the Atlantic to the Pacific and back again.

Amelia dove into her duties at *Cosmopolitan*,
writing articles about aviation and answering

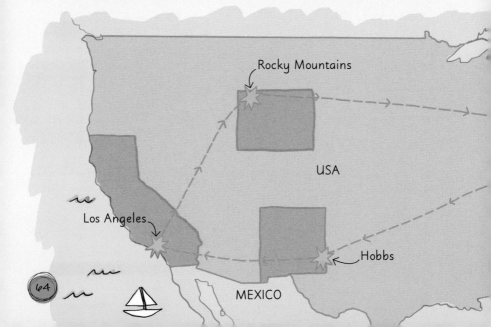

Rocky Mountains

USA

Los Angeles

Hobbs

MEXICO

letters from people curious about her or wanting to learn how to fly. She wanted to maintain some tie to social work, so she moved into Greenwich House, a settlement house in New York City. And then, as always, she began to wonder … what's next?

One thing not on the immediate horizon was marriage. Distance and Amelia's busy schedule meant that she and her fiancé, Sam, drifted apart. On November 22, 1928, Amelia announced in an interview that she had ended her engagement to Sam. They remained close friends for the rest of Amelia's life.

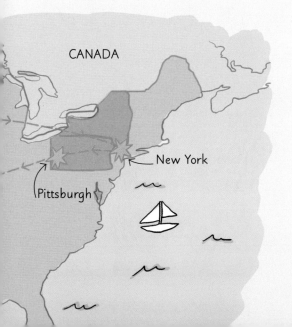

CANADA

New York

Pittsburgh

Chapter 8

Love, guts, and glory

In 1929, the National Air Races and Aeronautical Exposition announced that it would host a Women's Air Derby. Amelia entered the race.

The women would fly 2,350 miles (3,782 km) from Santa Monica, California, to Cleveland, Ohio. The winner would receive thousands of dollars in prize money. This was a first, and organizers soon began to worry. There would be bad publicity if a woman got killed! Their solution—each woman must take a male

Amelia (fourth from left) poses with a group of fliers during the first Women's Air Derby.

navigator along with her. This, of course, didn't sit well with the fliers. Amelia announced that no women would enter the race unless they could fly alone, and the idea was dropped.

To be competitive, Amelia needed a bigger, more powerful plane. She sold her little airplane and bought a Lockheed Vega. The sleek, streamlined aircraft was built for speed, but it was much bigger than anything Amelia had ever flown before. She had just five months to learn how to master its controls.

On August 18, all 19 women took to the air. Over the next nine days, newspapers reported on accidents, fires, and even one death. Amelia had her share of headlines, including an overshot landing that resulted in a bent—and quickly repaired—propeller. In the end, 16 women crossed the finish line. Amelia, who finished third, was quick to point out that this was the highest percentage of finishers in any cross-country event—for men or women—at the time.

In addition to showcasing women's aeronautical talents, the derby was a great place to build interest in the new flying organization, just for women, that Amelia and aviation pioneer Ruth Nichols had been discussing for the past two years. All of the finishers decided that its time had come. Letters were sent to each of the 117 licensed female pilots, and 99 joined the new group. In honor of the founding members, they called it The Ninety-Nines. When the group became more organized two years later, Amelia was elected as its first president.

Amelia was a very busy woman. In addition to The Ninety-Nines, she was still writing for *Cosmopolitan*, giving lectures, working for a

THE NINETY-NINES

The Ninety-Nines is an international organization that now represents thousands of female pilots from 44 countries. The group owns and manages the Amelia Earhart Birthplace Museum, in the house once owned by Amelia's grandparents in Atchison, Kansas. It also awards a scholarship in Amelia's name each year.

The first official meeting of The Ninety-Nines was held on November 2, 1929.

transcontinental airline company overseeing female passengers' needs, and she had a mountain of correspondence to keep up with. She hired a secretary, Norah Alsterlund, to help out. She also traded her Vega for a more powerful model and went about setting new women's speed and altitude records.

Amelia didn't want to be an ordinary bride and George never expected that she would be.

And then there was George. With Sam out of the picture, Amelia and George had grown very close. Just weeks after the Women's Air Derby, Dorothy packed her bags and moved out of their Rye home during a party—where Amelia was a guest. George and Dorothy divorced in December 1929, and George immediately began asking Amelia to marry him. It took nearly a year for Amelia to say yes.

Amelia married George on February 7, 1931. The ceremony lasted only five minutes. Worried about losing her independence, she handed George a note before the ceremony. It read: "I must exact a cruel promise, and that is you will let me go in a year if we find no happiness together." He agreed.

After the wedding, Amelia and George returned to Rye. She quickly went back to work, and her flying literally took on a new direction. Amelia became a test pilot for a new type of aircraft called the autogiro.

The autogiro was an intriguing new idea— an aircraft that could lift straight off the ground—and Amelia was sold. After setting an altitude record of 18,415 ft (5,613 m), she decided to become the first person to fly one from coast to coast. Unfortunately, after completing the first half of the challenge, she learned that another autogiro pilot had made the same trip a week before.

WHAT IS AN AUTOGIRO?

The autogiro, invented in 1923, was an early version of the helicopter. It looked a little like an airplane, but with a propeller in front to move the aircraft forward and one on top to create lift. It was very difficult to control in flight.

L'AUTOGYRE.

Between that disappointment and three crashes, Amelia's new fascination came to an end.

After that, Amelia began to write her second book. To boost sales, she waited to write the last chapter until she had completed her next adventure: flying solo across the Atlantic. Amelia had never felt like she deserved all the attention she got for her first transatlantic flight. After all, she had only been a passenger. Now, she wanted to prove that she could make the trip on her own as a pilot. And, she wanted to be the first woman to do it. Several other women were also preparing for the challenge, so Amelia and George kept their plans secret.

George hired experts to modify Amelia's plane so it could fly the distance. Then, they tested everything over and over again to ensure it all worked. Finally, they picked a date. The goal was to depart from Harbour Grace, Newfoundland, on May 20, 1932—exactly

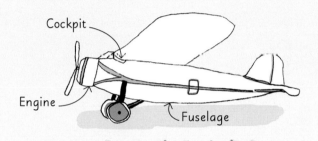
five years after Charles Lindbergh had set off on his successful transatlantic trip.

When the day finally arrived, Amelia, carrying cans of tomato juice and a thermos of soup, climbed into her Vega and posed for a few pictures. Then, at 7:12 p.m., she was off. If all went well, Paris would be her next stop.

For the first few hours, the skies were so clear that Amelia, cruising at an altitude of 12,000 ft (3,600 m), could see icebergs and fishing boats in the ocean below. But then, the plane's altimeter stopped working. Without that instrument, Amelia couldn't tell how high she was flying in the darkness. Fortunately, visibility was still pretty good, so Amelia reassured herself and focused her eyes on the job ahead. Then, Amelia smelled something burning. A small blue flame was flickering in her engine. The flame wasn't spreading, so Amelia decided it was safer to keep flying than to turn back and try to land with a plane full of gasoline.

So, she pressed on, and flew right into a storm. The thick black clouds were too tall for Amelia to fly over, and as rain turned to ice, the windshield and controls froze over. The plane went into a spin. After she dropped low enough for warmer temperatures to melt the ice, Amelia regained control. To avoid freezing up again, she flew just above the ocean's breaking waves for the rest of the night.

By daybreak, the storm had ended so Amelia climbed to fly above the puffy, white clouds. But her problems weren't over.

Gasoline began to leak from overhead and it was trickling down the side of her neck. Amelia had to land as soon as possible.

In the distance, Amelia spotted an open meadow, circled it twice, and landed. Rather than cheering crowds in Paris, she was greeted by a confused Irish farmer and his cows in a pasture just north of Londonderry (also called Derry), Northern Ireland. She had been in the air for 15 hours. Amelia spent the night with the farmer and his family and flew to London the next day, where a massive crowd of fans waited to see her.

DID YOU KNOW?

The US Congress awarded Amelia the Distinguished Flying Cross. She was the first woman to receive this medal.

9

New horizons

Amelia had proven herself to the world. She had also discovered something about herself. She could fly long distances, solo.

It was time to set new records! On July 1, 1932, just 10 days after returning to the US, Amelia set a new women's speed record for flying from Los Angeles to Newark, New Jersey: 19 hours, 14 minutes. She only stopped once. A few months later, she repeated the flight, nonstop this time, and cut her time by seven minutes. With that flight, she also became the first woman to fly nonstop coast to coast.

Next up was the third annual Bendix race, a cross-country free-for-all that started in New York and ended at the National Air Races in Los Angeles.

THE LITTLE RED BUS

Before she could compete in the Bendix race, Amelia had to get a new airplane. She had sold the Vega she had flown across the US and the Atlantic—except for the engine—to the Franklin Institute in Philadelphia for $7,500. Amelia painted that plane bright red and called it her "Little Red Bus." In 1966, the Little Red Bus found a new home—the Smithsonian Institution in Washington, D.C.

Just one month before the race date, sponsors announced that women would be allowed to compete for the first time. The male contestants flew more powerful planes and they had had

months to prepare for the competition, so Amelia knew she had no chance of winning—but she knew she had to try. On race day, Amelia was the first pilot to hit the air. But midway through the route, just west of Wichita, Kansas, strong headwinds caused her airplane's motor to heat up. She was forced to land and spent the night on the ground. The next day, the hatch cover of her plane blew open and she had to land again to get it repaired.

By the time Amelia finally arrived in Los Angeles, another contest was underway and she had to circle the airfield for an hour before it was safe to land. Amelia hadn't finished by the 6 p.m. race deadline, but she had finished and she won $2,000 for being the first woman to complete the race.

Amelia's constant quest for records was increasing her already enormous circle of admirers. Many of the women she had included in her "Activities of Women" scrapbook long ago were now fans. In November 1932, she met one of her greatest admirers—Eleanor Roosevelt— wife of the newly elected US president, Franklin D. Roosevelt.

Amelia and the president's wife had much in common, including their interest in social work, and became good friends. One evening, following a dinner at the White House, Amelia invited

Eleanor and Franklin D. Roosevelt

Mrs. Roosevelt—who had never flown at night before—to go on a nighttime flight over Washington, D.C. The women flew over the city still wearing the silk evening gowns and long white gloves they had worn earlier at the dinner.

Everyone wanted to know "Lady Lindy," and everyone wanted to look like her, too. So Amelia, who had already designed flying clothes for The Ninety-Nines, started her own clothing company. Her collection, which was sold exclusively at upscale department stores, was designed for women who lived active lives.

CLOTHING COMPANY

Amelia was one of the first celebrities to create her own fashion line. Working with her own sewing machine and a dressmaker's dummy, she designed simple, practical clothes. She also introduced the idea of matching "separates," which allowed customers to buy separate pieces of a suit in different sizes. Many of her pieces, including blouses made from parachute silk, had an aeronautical theme.

Amelia makes final adjustments to a sleeve.

However, the fashion industry is competitive and Amelia wasn't one to do anything halfway. After a year of trying to do it all—fly, write, lecture, lead The Ninety-Nines, and manage a clothing line—she had to drop something, and her venture into fashion came to an end.

People could no longer dress in Amelia's clothes, but they certainly could hear her story. Amelia was a popular speaker at events all around the world. Giving lectures was important because these speaking engagements were what truly paid the bills. Amelia often gave two speeches in one day at $300 per lecture.

But fame is fleeting, and Amelia knew the only way to attract big crowds was to do extraordinary things. So, she decided to pursue the one last great "first" that no man or woman had tackled so far. She was going to fly from Hawaii to California, across the Pacific Ocean.

Amelia wanted to keep
this trip a secret, but after
she and George left their new
Hollywood home in California and set sail
for Hawaii—along with a mechanic and a
few others—reporters knew something was
happening. George begrudgingly admitted that
Amelia might be flying back.

At 4:30 p.m. on January 11, 1935, Amelia
lifted off from Honolulu, the capital of Hawaii.
This flight was to be very different from her
Atlantic crossing. For one, she had a new two-way
radio in her cockpit. George had insisted that
Amelia stay in contact, so at a quarter to and
a quarter past each hour, she called out,
"Everything is OK." And every time a ship
along her route spotted her, it radioed her
position to the world.

Another big difference was the weather.
Instead of storms, Amelia experienced a night

What is a
two-way
radio?

A two-way radio is a device, like
a walkie-talkie, that lets people talk
with each other within a certain range.

of stars and tropical loveliness. After an uneventful flight of 18 hours, 16 minutes, Amelia landed in Oakland, California, where more than 10,000 people waited to greet her.

After this trip, Amelia was eager to go on another long-distance jaunt. So, as the moon shone on the evening of April 19, 1935, she took off from Los Angeles and headed for Mexico City. It was an easy trip until a bug flew in her eye and she couldn't read her map.

Amelia landed on a flat, dry lakebed in rural Mexico and was greeted by several local residents. She needed help, but they spoke only Spanish, and Amelia spoke only English, and they couldn't understand each other.

But after looking at her map, the people were able to point Amelia in the right direction. Some cowboys cleared all children and livestock out of the way and Amelia took off again, landing in Mexico City half an hour later. Amelia was the first person to make this 1,000-mile (1,600-km) trip alone.

Now, all Amelia had to do was make her way home and, possibly on a dare, she chose the most hazardous route for someone flying a single-engine aircraft. She shot straight out over the Gulf of Mexico—700 miles (1,130 km) of it—and she kept going.

A crowd had gathered at an airport in Washington, D.C.,

Honolulu

thinking Amelia would land there. Charles Lindbergh had stopped there when he had flown the same route from Mexico City seven years earlier. It took him 27 hours. Amelia roared past the airport in just 13 hours, six minutes. She kept going all the way to Newark, New Jersey. It was another record for someone flying solo.

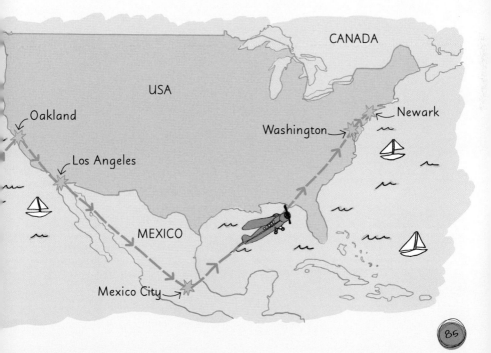

Amelia's big idea

Despite Amelia's success—and that of other female pilots—many people still thought women were less capable than men.

Amelia strongly disagreed. So, when Edward C. Elliott, president of Purdue University in Indiana, asked her to work at the school, she jumped at the opportunity. She would spend at least one month a year serving as a career counselor for female students and would become a technical adviser in aeronautics.

In her new role, Amelia tried to identify barriers for women and to teach her students how to overcome them. She urged them to graduate and establish themselves in a career before getting married.

This attitude made her popular with her students, but not with male staff and students on campus. They didn't think women should be competing for the same jobs as men, especially when there weren't a lot of jobs to be had. Plus, as one male student reasoned, it was hard enough to get the girls to agree to marry them in the first place!

Amelia's new position did not mean she had to give up flying. In 1935, she flew in the Bendix race once again. This time, she flew with fellow pilot and technical adviser, Paul Mantz. They placed fifth and won $500.

Two days after the Bendix, Laura Ingalls, an aviatrix from New York, flew nonstop coast-to-coast in just 13 hours, 35 minutes, smashing Amelia's record by more than five and a half hours.

Amelia with Paul Mantz

Laura Ingalls

Ingalls was flying a new airplane. Amelia knew that if she wanted to remain competitive, she would need a new plane, too, and she knew exactly what she wanted—a Lockheed Electra.

Fortunately for Amelia, George was a good listener and a master publicist as well. He relayed her

THE ELECTRA

The Electra was unlike any other plane at the time. It was an all-metal, twin-engine airliner with retractable landing gear that folded away during flight. The plane could hold 12 people. It was big—almost 39 ft (12 m) long, just over 10 ft (3 m) high, with a 55-ft (17-m) wingspan. It could soar up to 19,000 ft (5,800 m) high and fly up to 4,000 miles (6,400 km) without refueling. But at $80,000, it was also extremely expensive.

wish to President Elliott at Purdue, and also suggested creating a flying laboratory so Amelia could test the effects of air travel.

Elliott liked the idea and arranged a dinner party with Amelia and some of the university's wealthy alumni (former students), who were also members of the Purdue Research Foundation. Amelia shared her dream of a flying laboratory and they, too, were captivated by the idea. Before the night was over, alumni J. K. Lilly Sr. and David Ross had donated $50,000 to the cause. Later on, several companies donated thousands more in cash and equipment.

The Purdue Research Foundation was an innovative idea that created a link between Purdue University research laboratories and Indiana industries. All involved benefited from the arrangement. University researchers shared their knowledge, and wealthy alumni donated land and funds to build facilities including dormitories, an on-campus airport, and a new sports stadium. This development attracted wealth, attention, and students to the school.

On April 19, 1936, President Elliott announced the creation of the Amelia Earhart Fund for Aeronautical Research. Its first purchase was a Lockheed Electra. But before the plane could be delivered, it had to be customized to suit its new purpose. The engineers removed the passenger windows and seats and installed extra gas tanks in the cabin and a navigator's station behind them. They also added an autopilot system, deicing equipment, a radio that transmitted at three frequencies, and a radio direction finder, which enabled navigators to find their way using radio signals from the ground.

With her new plane in hand, another idea that had been brewing in Amelia's mind was now possible. She wanted to fly around the world. It had been done before, but not the way Amelia intended. She wanted to take the longest way possible, flying around the equator.

AMELIA'S NEW RADIO

The radio installed in Amelia's Electra transmitted at three frequencies—500, 3105, and 6210 kHz. At the time, ships used the lower frequency, 500 kHz, to transmit emergency messages via Morse code, a system of dots and dashes used in telecommunication. The radio direction finder also worked best on this frequency. But Amelia wasn't proficient in Morse code, so she didn't use this frequency. She used the highest frequency, 6210 kHz, to send voice messages.

Tackling this 27,000-mile (43,500-km) challenge, she said, would be "my frosting on the cake."

Amelia wasn't the only one excited about this grand idea. Purdue liked it, too, announcing that the flight would "develop scientific and engineering data of vital importance to the aviation industry." Purdue granted Amelia formal leave from the university, and preparations for her grand tour began.

George was in charge of logistics. With the extra fuel tanks on board,

what is the equator?

The equator is an imaginary line around the center of the Earth.

Amelia's Electra exceeded maximum weight restrictions for a commercial aircraft. So he had the US State Department contact each country on Amelia's route to have her plane certified as airworthy and grant her permission to fly over or land within their borders.

George also arranged for gas and oil to be available at up to 30 stops along the way. Amelia's plane would need to be overhauled several times, so he also had parts and mechanics stationed at strategic points along her route. One more duty George took on was keeping Amelia's worried family informed about her progress.

One massive problem remained. No matter which route Amelia took, it was impossible for her to fly over the vast Pacific Ocean without refueling. Their first idea was to have Amelia refuel in the air over Midway Island. George contacted the US Navy for help, and Amelia—not wanting to take any chances—wrote to President Roosevelt, too.

DID YOU KNOW?

The Sultanate of Muscat in the Arabian Peninsula was the only state that refused to let Amelia fly over its borders.

With Roosevelt's backing, the Navy agreed, as long as Amelia had special training to learn the procedure and paid all expenses.

Soon a different option emerged. With help from Amelia's close friend Gene Vidal, director of the Bureau of Air Commerce, and funding approved by President Roosevelt, an airstrip was built on Howland Island, a tiny speck of land that lay within flying distance of both New Guinea and Hawaii. Seeing this as the best choice, that's what the team decided to do.

Amelia with Eugene "Gene" Vidal, March 3, 1937.

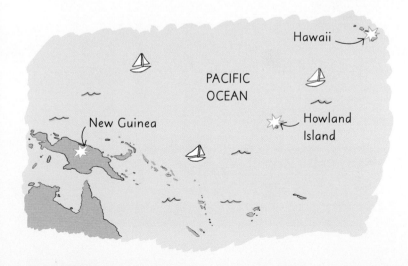

Hawaii

PACIFIC OCEAN

New Guinea

Howland Island

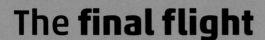
The **final flight**

Early in 1937, all of the pieces of Amelia's giant puzzle were finally in place. Unfortunately, the adventure got off to a rocky start.

On March 17, the plane flew from Oakland, California, to Honolulu, Hawaii. Joining Amelia were Harry Manning, her chief navigator, and Fred Noonan, a former Pan American Airways navigator who was an expert at celestial navigation.

From left to right: Harry, Amelia, Fred, and Paul had great hopes for the crew's around-the-world trip. Sadly, things didn't go as planned.

By looking at the stars, he could keep them on course. He would join them as far as Howland Island. In addition, Paul Mantz, Amelia's technical adviser, was on board to work out any final glitches. He would get off after they reached Hawaii.

At the crack of dawn two days later, they took off from Honolulu. With Amelia at the controls, the plane roared down the runway. Suddenly, its right wing dipped. Attempting to correct the situation, Amelia decreased power to the left engine, but that caused the plane to swing out of control. The landing gear collapsed, and sparks flew as the plane slid down the runway on its belly.

To prevent a fire, Amelia quickly shut down the engines, but the damage had been done. The right wing, both engine housings, the right-hand rudder, both propellers, and the underside of the fuselage were all seriously damaged. The oil tanks had also ruptured. The plane was shipped back to California for repairs.

Amelia and George studying a map the night before she attempted to fly around the world, in March 1937.

The team had to raise funds to keep the project going, and once again special stamps came to the rescue. Amelia signed 5,000 of them, which she would take on her trip. They also had to start planning all over again, and this time, there would be some major changes. Harry Manning—who had taken a leave from his job to join Amelia on the first try—could no longer go. Fred Noonan would now be her only navigator. In addition, Amelia decided to reverse her route to fly from west to east.

Flying the other direction had some major advantages. Because they were starting later

A COSTLY MISTAKE?

Neither Amelia nor Fred were proficient at Morse code. Rather than bring along a radio expert with those skills, Amelia had the 500 kHz trailing wire and the Morse code equipment removed from her plane, considering them to be unnecessary extra weight.

Morse code is a way of coding messages.

in the year, this was the only way they could reach the Caribbean and Africa before the monsoon season began, bringing heavy rains. The change put prevailing winds behind Amelia so she didn't have to fly into headwinds (winds blowing against you). But reversing course also meant that the difficult task of finding and landing on Howland Island would come at the end of the journey instead of the beginning.

On May 20, 1937, Amelia, George, Fred, and a mechanic left Oakland and headed for

what are prevailing winds? Wind blows from different directions. Prevailing winds are the main winds that usually blow from a particular direction in an area.

Miami, Florida. Mechanics worked on the plane for a week to work out any final bugs that remained after the accident. On June 1, everything was ready, and at 6:04 a.m., the Electra and its crew were off.

The first legs of the trip were easy. It took about eight hours for Amelia and Fred to reach San Juan, Puerto Rico. The next morning, they flew to Venezuela, and the day after that they resumed their trek, flying over dense jungles as they took the most direct route down the South American coast.

Then, it was time for the long hop over the South Atlantic, and at 3:15 a.m. on June 7, they left Brazil and headed for Dakar, French West Africa (today called Senegal). But as they closed in on the African coast, a thick haze blocked their view. Amelia ignored her navigator's advice to head south and landed in St. Louis, French West Africa, 165 miles (265 km) north of Dakar, instead.

George and Amelia used their entire life savings to finance her around-the-world trip.

The next morning, they got back on course and resumed their trek across Africa, with stops in what are now known as Dakar, Mali, Chad, Sudan, and Ethiopia. At one point, they flew low enough to see a herd of hippos in the river below. At another, it was so hot that the ground crew had to wait until after sunset to refuel their plane. And one airfield they visited was surrounded by a massive thorn hedge, built to keep out all the wild animals that lived around the airfield. Amelia felt like she was living a real-life version of the Bogie game she had played so long ago!

With Africa behind them, Amelia and Fred had a long nonstop flight to their next destination, Karachi (then in India, but now in Pakistan). So far, as she reported to

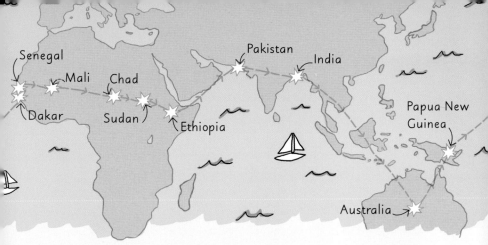

George back home, everything was going like clockwork. But the late start came to haunt them as they approached Calcutta (now Kolkata), India. Monsoon season had arrived, and heavy rains had turned the landing strip into a runway of mud.

Advised that the rains would only get worse, Amelia left at dawn the next day. She and Fred continued to battle heavy rains for the next two days. Finally, the sun broke through and they were flying without issues once again. They made their way through Southeast Asia to Australia, where all nonessential items—except for the stamp covers—were boxed up and sent home.

At dawn on June 29, Amelia and Fred set off for Lae, New Guinea (now Papua New Guinea), a 1,200-mile (1,900-km) flight, mostly over water.

They spent several days there, where the plane was serviced and more problems with the radio were fixed. Amelia and Fred studied maps and charts, knowing that with just 7,000 miles (11,300 km) left, their most difficult task lay ahead. On their next leg, they had to find tiny Howland Island … They never did.

"When I go, I'd like best to go in my plane. Quickly."

Amelia Earhart,
May 31, 1937

103

Chapter 12

Missing!

At 10 a.m. local time on July 2, 1937, Amelia taxied the Electra down the runway and headed for Howland Island.

Everything on Howland Island was ready and waiting for her arrival. Birds had been cleared from the runways, and a small house that had been built to accommodate her was given a final cleaning. The US Coast Guard cutter *Itasca* was stationed at Howland, ready to guide her in.

Fourteen hours and 15 minutes after Amelia had departed Lae, the *Itasca* picked up its first garbled voice message from her.

A cutter is a US Coast Guard vessel at least 65 ft (19.8 m) long, with space for crew to live.

The only words the crew could understand clearly were "cloudy weather." Amelia continued to send messages every half hour and while her voice was clear, her words were worrisome. At one point,

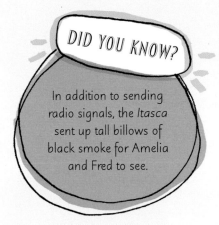

she reported that they were flying at 1,000 ft (300 m) and their gas was running low. She thought they were near the island, but they couldn't see it and hadn't received any transmissions from the ship.

The *Itasca*, in fact, had been sending a regular stream of weather reports and messages, but on bandwidths that Amelia's plane couldn't receive. The radio direction finder on Howland wouldn't work with Amelia's because they were operating on different bandwidths.

A tragic series of events involving human error, faulty equipment, and miscommunication made it impossible for Amelia to reach her would-be rescuers. Amelia sent one last message,

DAILY NEWS FINAL

EARHART PLANE LOST AT SEA

Amelia Earhart Missing on World Flight

People around the world read about Amelia's disappearance.

20 hours and 14 minutes into her flight, and then there was silence.

The search began. For the next 16 days, with the US Navy and Coast Guard in charge, 66 aircraft and nine ships scoured the ocean and nearby islands looking for Amelia and Fred. People all over the world monitored the airwaves, hoping to hear Amelia's voice. And many people—both members of the military and amateur radio operators—reported hearing her pleas for help.

After the official search ended on July 18, 1937, George financed the search himself. But nobody could find her. Amelia was officially declared dead on January 5, 1939. However, the search for

Amelia Earhart has never ended. Decades later, people are still looking for her plane, her remains, and an answer to one of the greatest aviation mysteries of all time.

Over the years, several theories have emerged. Some people believe that Amelia's plane crashed into the sea. Up to now, multiple searches of the seafloor with high-tech, deep-sea sonar equipment have found no evidence of this. Another theory is that Amelia and Fred crashed on a nearby uninhabited island and lived the rest of their lives as castaways. Nikumaroro, which at the time was called Gardner Island and lies about 350 miles

(560 km) from Howland Island, was the likely location. Artifacts including human remains and plane parts resembling those of Amelia's Electra have been discovered there, but so far nothing has been proven.

HILARY SWANK   RICHARD GERE

Amelia

COMING SOON

Amelia's life still shines on the big screen.

One thing that is known for sure is that, now, Amelia is gone. But her name and her legacy have not been forgotten. Movies have been made about her life and books have been written. A residence hall and café at Purdue University bear her name, and The Ninety-Nines, which she helped found, still flourishes. To this day, Amelia continues to inspire for her courage, her spirit, and her heart-felt belief that anyone can accomplish their goals if they are simply given the opportunity to try.

Amelia's
family tree

Grandfather

Rev. David
Earhart
1818–1903

Grandmother

Mary Wells
1821–1893

Father

Edwin Earhart
1867–1930

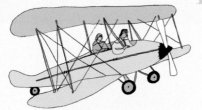

Husband

George Palmer
Putnam
1887–1950

↳ Putnam belonged
to a powerful family
of publishers.

Grandfather

Alfred Otis
1827–1912

Grandmother

Amelia Harres
1837–1912

Mother

Amy Otis
1869–1962

Sister

Muriel Earhart
1899–1998

Amelia Earhart
1897–1939*

*This was when Amelia was officially declared dead. However, nobody knows for sure when Amelia died.

Timeline

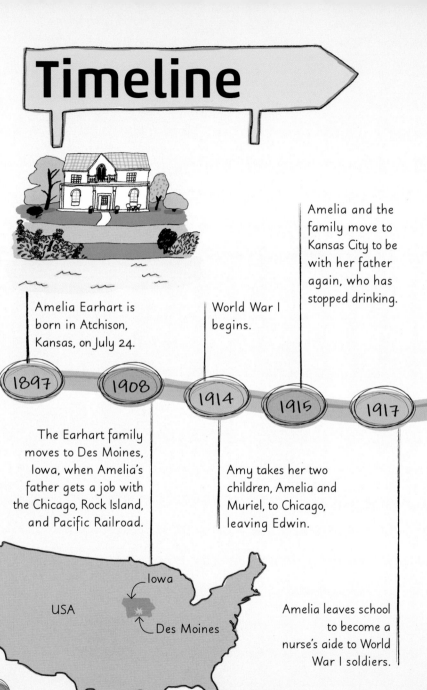

Amelia Earhart is born in Atchison, Kansas, on July 24.

World War I begins.

Amelia and the family move to Kansas City to be with her father again, who has stopped drinking.

1897

1908

1914

1915

1917

The Earhart family moves to Des Moines, Iowa, when Amelia's father gets a job with the Chicago, Rock Island, and Pacific Railroad.

Amy takes her two children, Amelia and Muriel, to Chicago, leaving Edwin.

Iowa

USA

Des Moines

Amelia leaves school to become a nurse's aide to World War I soldiers.

Amelia's parents divorce. While her father stays in California, Amelia and the rest of the family move back to the East Coast.

Amelia takes her first solo flight and starts participating in air meets.

Amelia takes her first flying lesson with Neta Snook on January 3.

1921   1922   1923   1924   1926

Amelia buys a yellow plane, calling it "the Canary."

Amelia is hired as a social worker at Denison House in Boston, Massachusetts.

Amelia sets a new altitude record for female pilots at 14,000 ft (4,300 m) on October 22.

Amelia becomes the 16th woman to earn a pilot's license from the Fédération Aéronautique Internationale on May 16.

Amelia becomes the first woman to fly nonstop coast to coast, setting a women's speed record from Los Angeles to Newark, New Jersey.

The *Friendship*, with captain Amelia Earhart, makes a 20-hour flight across the Atlantic Ocean, landing in Wales.

On November 2, the first meeting of The Ninety-Nines, the organization for female pilots that Amelia helped found, is held.

1928

1929

1931

1932

On September 14, Amelia arrives in Los Angeles from New York, successfully completing her solo cross-country flight. She then flies back to New York.

Amelia and George Putnam marry on February 7.

Amelia becomes the first woman to fly solo across the Atlantic.

Amelia competes in the first Women's Air Derby.

On January 11, Amelia flies from Honolulu, becoming the first person to cross the Pacific back to California.

On March 17, Amelia and her crew begin their first, failed, attempt to fly around the world. On June 1, Amelia and navigator Fred Noonan begin their second attempt.

On July 2, Amelia and Fred depart Lae, heading for Howland Island. They disappear.

Amelia is officially declared dead on January 5.

1935

1937

1939

On June 29, Amelia and Fred arrive in Lae, New Guinea (now Papua New Guinea).

The official search for Amelia and Fred ends on July 18.

On April 19, Amelia flies from California to Mexico City, the first person to make this trip alone.

Quiz

What was the name of the game Amelia and her childhood friends invented that had them traveling on imaginary trips around the world?

How old was Amelia when she saw an airplane for the first time at the Iowa State Fair?

What job did Amelia leave school to do during World War I?

What did Amelia wear to her first flying lesson?

Where was Amelia working and training to be a social worker?

Why was the *Friendship* painted gold and orange?

To whom did Amelia dedicate her first book, *20 hrs. 40 min.: Our flight in the Friendship*?

**Do you remember what you've read?
How many of these questions about
Amelia's life can you answer?**

 8 How did The Ninety-Nines get its name?

 9 What did Amelia and Eleanor Roosevelt wear on their nighttime flight over Washington, D.C.?

 10 What kind of new plane did Amelia buy with money raised by the Amelia Earhart Fund for Aeronautical Research?

 11 What did Amelia do with the Morse code equipment in her plane?

 12 What was the name of the Coast Guard boat waiting to guide Amelia to Howland Island?

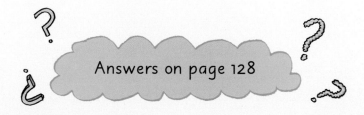

Answers on page 128

Who's who?

Alsterlund, Norah
(1905–1996) Amelia's
secretary

Boll, Mabel
(1893–1949) adventurer
nicknamed the "Queen
of Diamonds"

Byrd, Richard E.
(1888–1957) explorer
who flew around the
North Pole

Chapman, Sam
(unknown) Amelia's fiancé

Coolidge, Calvin
(1872–1933) president of
the United States from
1923 to 1929

Elliott, Edward C.
(1874–1960) president
of Purdue University

Gordon, Lou
(1897–1938) mechanic
on the *Friendship*
during Amelia's first
transatlantic flight

Guest, Amy Phipps
(1872–1959) wealthy
socialite who hired
Amelia to captain her
plane across the Atlantic

Hawks, Frank
(1897–1938) air race pilot
who gave Amelia her first
ride in an airplane

Heath, Lady Mary
(1896–1939) British
pilot who sold Amelia
an airplane

Ingalls, Laura
(1893–1967) pilot who broke
Amelia's nonstop coast-to-
coast flight record in 1935

Lindbergh, Charles
(1902–1974) first pilot to
make a solo flight across
the Atlantic Ocean

Manning, Harry
(1897–1974) Amelia's
chief navigator on her
first attempt at flying
around the world

Mantz, Paul
(1903–1965) Amelia's fellow
pilot and technical adviser

Montijo, John
(1891–1935) ex-Army
pilot who taught Amelia
stunt flying

Nichols, Ruth
(1901–1960) one of the
cofounders, with Amelia, of
The Ninety-Nines, a flying
organization for women

Noonan, Fred
(1893–1937) navigator,
lost with Amelia, on her
attempted flight around
the world

Putnam, Dorothy
(1888–1982) Amelia's
friend and George
Putnam's first wife

**Putnam, George
Palmer**
(1887–1950) Amelia's
husband and promoter

Railey, Hilton
(1895–1975) public
relations specialist who
helped connect Amelia
with Amy Phipps Guest

Rasche, Thea
(1899–1971) German
stunt pilot

Roosevelt, Eleanor
(1884–1962) first lady
of the United States from
1933 to 1945, married
to Franklin D. Roosevelt

Roosevelt, Franklin D.
(1882–1945) president
of the United States from
1933 to 1945, married to
Eleanor Roosevelt

Snook, Neta
(1896–1991) Amelia's
first flying instructor

Stultz, Wilmer ("Bill")
(1900–1929) pilot of the
Friendship on Amelia's
first Atlantic crossing

Vidal, Eugene ("Gene")
(1895–1969) director of the
Bureau of Air Commerce
and friend to Amelia

Glossary

activist
person who protests for or against something they have a strong opinion about

aerial
in the air

aerial map
map made for pilots based on aerial photographs

aerobatics
spectacular tricks and maneuvers performed in the air

airstrip
runway where planes land without airport services

alcohol
strong drink, such as beer, wine, or whiskey, that can change a person's behavior

altitude
height above sea-level

alumni
former students or graduates of a particular school

armistice
truce between opposite sides in a war

autogiro
early version of a helicopter

autopilot
device that steers planes on its own

aviatrix
female pilot

bandwidth
range of radio frequencies
that a device can use to
send and receive messages

bloomers
wide, loose, knee-length pants

bluff
high, steep cliff that
overlooks a river, beach,
or other coastal area

boarder
someone who pays a family
to stay in their house and
eat meals with them

capable
able to do something

celestial
having to do with the sky

cockpit
part of the plane
where the pilot sits

credential
experience or skill that
means someone is able
to do a certain job

dominate
be more powerful

equator
imaginary line
around the center
of the Earth

expedition
trip with a specific goal

flying blind
relying on a plane's
instruments to fly
when visibility is low

fuselage
body of a plane

gushing
coming out quickly

hauling
moving or carrying
something heavy

horizon
where the sky and the Earth
meet in the distance

hubbub
loud mix of sound
and activity

latitude
imaginary lines used
for measurement that
circle the Earth parallel
to the equator

longitude
imaginary lines from the
North Pole to the South
Pole, used to measure
distance East and West

loop
aerial maneuver in which
an aircraft completes a
vertical circle

massive
huge

monsoon
season of storms with
heavy wind and rain in
the Indian Ocean and
southern Asia

navigation
finding the way from
one place to another

pampered
treated very well

parishioner
person who attends
a local church

pontoon
float on the bottom
of some planes that
lets them land and
take off from water

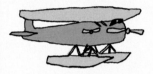

prevailing winds
main winds that usually
blow from a particular
direction in an area

propeller
turning blades that
make a plane move

psychologist
person who studies and
treats mental conditions

Red Cross
volunteer organization
that helps people around
the world who are facing
emergencies

roll
aerial maneuver in which
an aircraft turns over to
the left or right

rudder
part of the plane that the
pilot moves to steer left and
right; a rudder is also used
to steer boats

settlement house
place that provides
services to people
in a neighborhood

spin
aerial maneuver in which
a plane rotates on its axis
as it flies straight down

stunt
daring and difficult trick

taxi
steer an airplane on
the ground or on water

transatlantic
across the Atlantic Ocean

transmissions
signals or information that
are passed or sent to another
person or place

trench
long, narrow ditch dug
in the ground

two-way radio
device, like a walkie-talkie,
that lets people talk to each
other within a certain range

upgrading
moving up to a higher level

utterly
completely

vocation
work or occupation that
is important to a person

Index

Ee

Earhart, Amy (mother) 8,
9–10, 12, 18, 20–21, 22,
25, 29, 32, 37, 39, 40, 52
Earhart, David (grandfather)
9
Earhart, Edwin (father) 8–10,
13, 16–19, 20, 22, 29, 31,
32, 37, 39, 52
Earhart, Mary (grandmother)
9
Earhart, Muriel (sister) 10,
12, 13, 18, 19–20, 22,
25, 39, 40, 52
education 19–23, 29, 40, 41
Elliott, Edward C. 86, 89, 90
engineering 40
equator 90–91
Ethiopia 100

Ff

fame 56–61, 108
flight, Amelia's first 31–33
flu epidemic 29
flying, Amelia's fascination
with 27–28, 29
flying blind 52
flying laboratory 89–90
flying lessons 32–36
Ford, Henry 58
French West Africa 98

Friendship 47, 50–55, 56,
59, 60

Gg

Gordon, Lou 51
Guest, Amy Phipps 47–49, 58

Hh

hairstyle 35
Hawaii 81, 82, 84, 93, 94,
95
Hawks, Frank 31–33
health 29, 39–40
Heath, Lady Mary 58–59
Howland Island 93, 95,
97, 102, 104, 105

Ii

India 100, 101
Ingalls, Laura 87–88
inheritance 18, 22
Iowa State Fair 17
Itasca 104–105

Jj

jobs 37, 38, 40, 41–43

Kk

Kansas City 10, 13–14, 22
Kinner, Bert 35

Putnam, Dorothy 60, 61, 70
Putnam, George 48–49, 56,
    60–63, 70–71, 72, 82,
    88, 91–92, 97, 99, 106

Rr

radios 82, 90, 91, 97,
    104–106
Railey, Hilton 49, 56
Rasche, Thea 44–45, 53
Red Cross 24–25, 26
Roosevelt, Eleanor 78–79
Roosevelt, Franklin D.
    78–79, 92–93
Ross, David 89

Ss

St. Louis World Fair 14
St. Paul, Minnesota 19
settlement houses 41, 42, 65
sledding 13–14
smoke signals 105
Snook, Neta 33–36
social work 41–43, 65, 79
solo flight, first 36
speed record 69, 76
sports 12, 19, 21, 23, 42
Springfield, Missouri 20
stamps 84, 96, 101
Stultz, Wilmer "Bill" 51,
    53–55, 58
Sudan 100

Tt

Toronto 25, 26
transatlantic flights 46–55,
    58, 72–75
transport pilot's license 67
two-way radios 82

Uu

United States, flights across
    62–65, 76, 87
US Navy 92, 106

Vv

Venezuela 98
Vidal, Eugene ("Gene") 93

Ww

Washington, D.C. 79, 84
women, position of 86–87
Women's Air Derby 66–68,
    70
Women's Educational
    and Industrial Union
    (WEIU) 41
world, circumnavigation
    of 90–102
World War I 24–26

Acknowledgments

The author would like to thank: Her husband and sons for patiently listening every time she told them another cool fact she'd just learned about Amelia Earhart.

DK would like to thank: Caroline Hunt for proofreading; Helen Peters for the index; Abby Aitcheson, Cécile Landau, and Margaret Parrish for editorial help; and Maya Frank-Levine for writing the reference section.

ANSWERS TO THE QUIZ ON PAGES 116–117

1. Bogie; 2. 10; 3. nurse's aide; 4. her horseback riding outfit; 5. Denison House; 6. to make it easy to spot if it went down at sea; 7. Dorothy Putnam; 8. after the ninety-nine women who were the first members; 9. silk evening gowns and long white gloves; 10. Lockheed Electra; 11. she had it removed; 12. *Itasca*